GREAT EXPLORATIONS

Juan Ponce de León

Discoverer of Florida

Steven Otfinoski

Benchmark Books

MARSHALL CAVENDISH
NEW YORK

Benchmark Books
99 White Plains Road
Tarrytown, NY 10591-9001
www.marshallcavendish.com

Copyright © 2005 by Marshall Cavendish Corporation
Map copyright © 2005 by Marshall Cavendish Corporation
Map by Rodica Prato

Library of Congress Cataloging-in-Publication Data

Otfinoski, Steven.
Juan Ponce de Leon : discoverer of Florida / by Steven Otfinoski.
p. cm.—(Great explorations)
Includes bibliographical references and index.
Contents: The soldier's way—Westward with Columbus—The Governor of
Higüey—Father of Puerto Rico—The Fountain of Youth—An island
called Florida—The King's favorite—At war with the Carib—To die in Florida.
ISBN 0-7614-1610-2
1. Ponce de Leon, Juan, 1460?-1521—Juvenile literature. 2.Explorers—America—Biography—
Juvenile literature. 3.Explorers—Spain—Biography—Juvenile literature. 4. America—Discovery
and exploration—Spanish—Juvenile literature. 5. Florida—Discovery and exploration—
Spanish—Juvenile literature. [1. Ponce de Leon, Juan,
1460?-1521. 2. Explorers. 3. America—Discovery and
exploration—Spanish.] I. Title. II. Series.

E125.P7O84 2003
975.9'01'092—dc22

2003017582

Photo research by Candlepants Incorporated

Cover photo: Service Historique de la Marine, Vincennes, /Bridgeman Art Library
Cover inset: North Wind Picture Archive

The photographs in this book are used by permission and through the courtesy of: *Corbis:* Bettmann, 5;
Jeremy Horner, 63; Bob Krist, 64; Wolfgang Kaehler, 67. *The Art Archive*: Real Monasterio del
Escorial Spain/Dagli Orti , 9; Naval Museum Genoa/ Dagli Orti, 13; Eileen Tweedy, 21; Biblioteca d'Ajuda Lisbon/
Dagli Orti, 28; Biblioteca Nazionale Marciana Venice/Dagli Orti, 48; General Archive of the Indies Seville/ Dagli
Orti, 57. *Art Resource, NY*: Erich Lessing, 10; Image Select, 31; Alinari, 51. *North Wind Picture Archive*: 15, 18, 20,
23, 35, 38, 49, 58, 61. *Bridgeman Art Library*: Private Collection, 24, 42-43; Bibliotheque des Arts Decoratifs, Paris,
France/Archives Charmet, 45; Private Collection/Michael Graham-Stewart, 54.

Printed in China
1 3 5 6 4 2

Contents

foreword

Few legends from the Age of Exploration are as enduring or as captivating as the story of the Fountain of Youth. Just as Spanish explorer Francisco Coronado is forever linked with the fabled seven golden cities of Cíbola, so Juan Ponce de León will always be associated with the Fountain of Youth that he is said to have sought in Florida.

Yet the magical fountain played only a minor role in Ponce de León's eventful career. While it is true he never found it, he probably never looked very hard for it in the first place. The experienced Spanish soldier probably didn't even believe such a fountain existed.

The Fountain of Youth is just one of the misconceptions many people have associated with this most misunderstood of conquistadors. Ponce de León is popularly credited with founding the city of St. Augustine, the first permanent settlement in the United States. In fact, St. Augustine wasn't founded until nearly forty-five years after

Ponce de León is offered a glass of water from the fountain of Youth in this fanciful illustration.

Ponce de León's death. While he did discover and name Florida, he never established a colony there.

Ponce de León instead played a much bigger role in the founding and growth of two important islands in the West Indies—Hispaniola, which today comprises the nations of Haiti and the Dominican Republic—and Puerto Rico, where he served as the colony's first governor.

As a conquistador, Ponce de León was something of an oddity. He was one of the few who saw more wealth in the soil than in gold and silver. He excelled as a farmer as well as a soldier and took great pride in what he could grow from the land. While most conquistadors plundered and amassed great wealth, taking it back to Europe with them, Ponce de León set down roots in the New World, establishing a plantation and raising a family there. While his wealth was built on the backs of his Indian laborers, he generally treated the native residents better than the other Spaniards.

Although he never achieved his goal of settling the lovely but treacherous land he called *La Florida*, Ponce de León paved the way for others to explore the rich, new world of North America. This is his story.

ONE

The Soldier's Way

Of all the conquistadors who came to North and South America, perhaps none is as little known today as Juan Ponce de León. Many parts of his life—including his early and his final years—are poorly documented. The exact date of his birth is not even certain. Historians disagree on the year, placing it anywhere from 1460 to 1474. This last date may be the most accurate, as it is based on written testimony Ponce de León gave in a 1514 court case, in which he stated he was forty years old.

This lack of information may have resulted partly from the fact that Ponce de León was probably born out of wedlock. The names of his parents are unknown, but the Ponce de León family was an illustrious one in Spain. Don Rodrigo Ponce de León was a military hero in the wars against the Moors—Muslims from North Africa—in Granada. Another celebrated relative, Don Pedro Ponce de León, was the popular duke of Cadiz in southwestern Spain.

THE MOORS

The Moors were nomadic people of North Africa who were converted to Islam in the 700s. Through conquest, they spread their influence and control south into Saharan Africa and north into Europe. Charles Martel, king of the Franks and grandfather of Charlemagne, forced the Moors from France in 732. But by 756, they had established themselves in southern Spain. One by one, the great Spanish cities fell to the Moors—Toledo, Córdoba, and Seville among them.

The Christians of northern Spain gradually regained control of the region, beginning with Toledo in 1085. By the late 1400s, the Moors had been driven out of every part of the country but Granada. After their defeat in 1492, many Moors remained in Spain, some even converting to Christianity. But by 1614, they had been expelled, thus ending 900 years of Moorish influence in Spain.

The Moors deeply influenced their conquered territories. In addition to bringing Islam to Spain, they built great universities and added immeasurably to the world's knowledge of medicine and science. Their great legacy can still be seen in many parts of Spain today.

The battle between Moors and Christians for Spanish lands raged for hundreds of years. The skirmishes were often tightly fought, as this illustration from a thirteenth-century manuscript vividly shows.

The Soldier's Way

Juan came from a less renowned branch of the family. He was born in San Tervas de Campos, near the city of Valladolid in northern Spain. It is believed his parents died when he was very young. Eventually he was sent, like many Spanish boys, to serve a nobleman as a page, or personal servant. Juan went to the estate of Don Pedro Núñez de Guzmán, lord of Toral and knight commander of the Order of Calatrava. Guzmán was known for his skill in training soldiers. Under his tutelage, Ponce de León learned to ride, hunt, and fight in combat, all in preparation for becoming a soldier.

This detail from a Spanish painting shows knights training for a tournament. Young Ponce de León underwent similar preparation learning how to be an effective soldier in combat.

In the late 1400s, Spain was in need of good soldiers. The Moors had occupied Spain since the 700s. By 1482 their lands had been reduced to one stronghold—the province of Granada in southern Spain. For ten years, the Spaniards fought to drive them out. At the final battle of Granada in early 1492, the Moors were defeated and driven from Spanish soil. Ponce de León may have taken part in this fight as a young soldier of eighteen.

Another important event also took place in 1492. That October, an Italian navigator sailing for Spain reached a few tiny islands in the West Indies. Trying to find a sea route to the ports of the East, he mistakenly believed he was in Asia. Instead, Christopher Columbus had stumbled on the Americas. After this important discovery, Spain and the rest of Europe would never be the same again.

T W O

Westward with Columbus

Christopher Columbus returned from his historic voyage a hero. Spain's King Ferdinand and Queen Isabella, who had financed his trip, showered him with honors. Among the titles they bestowed on the explorer was admiral of the seas. The king and queen were now prepared to send Columbus back to the West Indies with a grand expedition that would establish settlements on the islands he had discovered. They also commissioned him to continue his search for the Asian mainland that he was convinced lay just beyond the Caribbean Sea.

On his first voyage, Columbus had commanded three ships. On his second, he would have no fewer than seventeen. Their crews were made up of sailors, soldiers, and settlers with various skills. Horses, cattle, goats, and pigs were also loaded on board to help provide food and labor for the new colonies.

Italian explorer Christopher Columbus made four voyages to the New World. Young Ponce de León may have accompanied him on his second voyage in 1493.

Some historians claim Ponce de León was one of the soldiers on Columbus's second voyage, but the evidence is not conclusive. The young soldier may have had some battle experience as a soldier in Guzmán's army. Whatever action he might have seen against the Moors would have held him in good stead as a protector of the settlers from the native peoples of the New World.

Columbus's fleet sailed from the port of Cadiz on September 25, 1493. Land was sighted on November 3. Because it was a Sunday, Columbus named the island they sighted *Dominica*, the Latin word for Sunday. The following day they anchored off the island of Guadeloupe. From there they sailed to Hispaniola, where Columbus had established a small settlement on his first voyage. About forty men had been left there to build fortifications and await his return. What Columbus found when he arrived in Hispaniola shocked him. The fort was in ruins, and there was no sign of any of the men he had left behind. Mystified, Columbus turned to the native inhabitants, who offered the explorer their version of what had happened. The Spaniards, they claimed, were struck with gold fever. They abandoned the work of building the new settlement and spent all their time hunting for gold. They took what gold the Indians had and then tried to force them to find more. But the Indians resisted and attacked the settlement, killing many of the settlers. Those who survived the attack fled into the forest where they soon perished.

Whether Columbus believed the Indians' story or not, he was careful not to punish them. He had orders from the king and queen to convert the natives to Christianity. So he let the missionaries in his party work among them while he turned his attention to establishing a new settlement in the northern part of the island. He called it *La Isabella* in honor of the queen. Ponce de León may have been among the soldiers stationed at *La Isabella* where a fort was eventually built.

Vibrant but historically inaccurate, this woodcut shows La Isabella, Columbus's first permanent settlement on Hispaniola. The grand castle on the left was in reality a simple wooden fort.

He also may have been among the Spanish party, led by Columbus, that first explored a number of new islands, including the Virgin Islands and Jamaica. Yet another island lay to the east of Hispaniola. Because they landed there on the feast day of John the Baptist, Columbus named it *San Juan Bautista*. Today it is known as Puerto Rico.

Columbus returned to Hispaniola to find that he had more to fear from the Spanish settlers than the Indians. They resented Columbus's strict discipline, forgetting what had become of those left behind when order broke down. The growing resentment of the Spaniards was more than Columbus could handle. In 1496 he decided to return to Spain to raise an army that would enforce law and order in Hispaniola.

Whether Ponce de León returned with him is not known. The truth is that the years between 1496 and 1502 are a complete blank in the conquistador's life. If he was on this voyage, he may have returned with Columbus and sailed back later on another ship. It is possible he remained on Hispaniola, but this seems unlikely.

One thing is certain: Ponce de León was not part of Columbus's ill-fated third voyage to the New World in 1498. This expedition ended in disaster. The newly appointed royal commissioner of Hispaniola, Francisco de Bobadilla, had Columbus arrested and sent the great explorer back to Spain in chains. Ponce de León probably returned to Hispaniola in 1502 as part of the party led by the new governor of the island, Nicolás de Ovando. That same year Columbus, who was later released in Spain, would return to the New World one last time with little success. Juan Ponce de León, however, would begin his rise to power and wealth on Hispaniola.

THREE

The Governor of Higüey

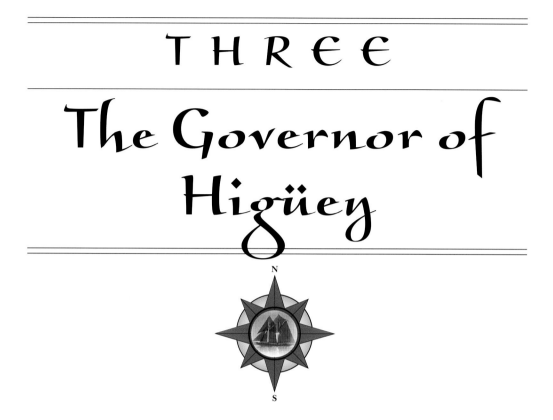

Hispaniola was a much different place in the spring of 1502 than when Ponce de León had first seen it in 1493. Santo Domingo, the capital, was by then a bustling town. Large farms called plantations stretched across the land in every direction. But one part of the island was still untamed and not under Spanish control. This was the southeastern province of Higüey, which is today part of the Dominican Republic. There the Arawak, or Taino, Indians remained in power and posed a serious threat to Spanish rule on the island.

Governor Ovando was determined to seize Higüey from the Indians and to bring it under Spanish control. In 1503 Juan de Esquivel led the main army in its attack on Higüey, defeating the Arawak. However, the Arawak rebelled again the next year, and Esquivel was once again sent to put down the uprising. Ponce de León followed with a second force from Santo Domingo. Although

This woodcut from 1572 shows some of the various fruit trees that thrived on Hispaniola. Agriculture was a key industry on the island, and vast plantations sprang up shortly after the Spanish established their presence there.

they were outnumbered four to one, the combined Spanish forces routed the Arawak.

Ponce de León's effective, if brutal, suppression of the rebellion made him a hero on the island. Governor Ovando rewarded him for his valor and leadership by making him *adelantado*, or frontier governor, of Higüey. Along with this position, Ponce de León was given a large land grant called an encomienda.

SANTO DOMINGO – FIRST CAPITAL OF SPANISH AMERICA

Santo Domingo was not the first settlement on Hispaniola, but it was the first that took root. *La Isabella*, founded by Columbus on the northern coast of the island, lasted only a short time. Santo Domingo, founded by his brother Bartholomew in 1496, slowly grew and today is the oldest continuously occupied European settlement in the Western Hemisphere.

It became the center of Spain's colonial administration in the New World and remained so for more than two decades. With the conquest of Mexico by Hernán Cortés in the 1520s and Peru by Francisco Pizarro in the 1530s, the base of power shifted to these new lands. But Santo Domingo remained an important stopping place for ships going to and from Spain.

Besides being the oldest settlement, Santo Domingo can also lay claim to having the oldest cathedral (1514) and the oldest university, the University of Santo Domingo (1538), in the hemisphere. Today this modern metropolis of more than a million people is the largest city in and leading port of the Dominican Republic.

Spanish soldiers take Indian prisoners under the watchful eye of Hispaniola's governor Nicolás de Ovando. Ponce de León played a major role in ending two Indian rebellions on the island.

Ponce de León did not go to Higüey alone. He had married since his arrival in Hispaniola. His bride's name was Leónor, but little else is known about her. It is believed that she was the daughter of an innkeeper in Santo Domingo. Together they had four children—three daughters, Juana, Isabel, and María, and a son, Luis. A strong woman, Leónor proved to be a valuable partner in the wilds of Higüey.

Few Spanish gentlemen would have considered Higüey a desirable prize. For one thing, it was not near Santo Domingo and its pleasures. For another, little gold had been found there. This didn't bother Ponce de León. For him the riches of the New World lay not in mineral wealth but in land. A born farmer, he cultivated cassava root, sweet potatoes, corn, bananas, and sugarcane on his plantation and raised cattle, horses, and pigs.

THE ENCOMIENDA SYSTEM

Ponce de León and many other Spaniards grew rich quickly in the New World due in large part to the encomienda system. This was a system of labor that was first used with the conquered Moors in Spain. In the New World, the encomienda system justified the seizing of Indians' lands. The valuable parcels were then given to those Spaniards favored by the king as a reward for their support and achievements. The Indians were still required to work the land and had to pay the new landowners tribute in the form of crops. In return, the landowners were to offer the Indians protection and instruction in the Christian faith. In reality, however, the Indians were treated like slaves, and many died from being overworked.

The injustices of the encomienda system eventually led to its reform by the king and such champions of the Indians as Friar Bartolomé de las Casas. The New Laws passed in 1542 were meant to improve the Indians' lives. Under the newly created repartimiento system they were considered free citizens of Spain and, while often required to work, were to be paid a wage.

But the Spanish officials in the New World abused this system just as they had the old one. Some Indians lived slightly better than before, but most suffered the same injustices.

This map of the island of Hispaniola was made in 1633 and shows the development of the colony after more than a century of Spanish rule.

Ponce de León was also a good businessman. He sold his produce to Spanish traders who then shipped it back to Spain. He quickly grew rich on his profits and built his family a large stone house, the only one of its kind in the province. Building such a sturdy and durable residence showed everyone that Juan Ponce de León had come to the New World to stay.

Under the governor's orders, Ponce de León built two towns in Higüey—Santa Cruz de Aycayague and Salvalon. He named this last town in honor of his maternal grandmother's estate back home in Spain.

Because Ponce de León treated his workers more humanely than the other landowners on Hispaniola, the Indians told him things that they did not tell the other Spaniards. One piece of information concerned an island to the east whose native residents often came to Hispaniola to trade their gold. They named it Boriquén, but the Spaniards called it San Juan Bautista. Since Ponce de León had explored the island with

Under the encomienda system, the harsh treatment of Indian laborers became all too common.

Columbus in 1493, it had not been revisited by Spanish ships. Boriquén was still controlled by its native peoples.

Ponce de León immediately asked Ovando for permission to explore the island and was granted the governor's approval. In 1506 Ponce de León led an expedition of five ships and about 200 men back to San Juan Bautista, which will be referred to by its present-day name, Puerto Rico.

F O U R

Father of Puerto Rico

Ponce de León landed in Puerto Rico on June 24, 1506, at the same spot on the western shore where Columbus had dropped anchor some thirteen years earlier. It was called *El Aguada*, which means "the watering hole," by later visitors because it was one of the best places to get fresh water on that part of the island.

Upon arrival, Ponce de León met and befriended the local chief of the Arawak Indians, Agüeybana. The Arawaks on Puerto Rico were a peaceful people who lived in fear of the Caribs, a group occupying the island's eastern end. The conquistador promised Agüeybana that he would help his people defeat the Caribs. To seal the agreement, gifts were exchanged, and Agüeybana invited the Spaniards to a great feast and pig hunt. Later the Arawaks took Ponce de León on a tour of the island. The conquistador liked what he saw. The island had fine harbors and was rumored to have rich deposits of gold, which he knew would please the king. Legend has it that when Ponce de León first laid eyes on the harbor on the northern coast near present-day San Juan he cried "!*Que puerto tan rico!*" meaning "What a rich port!" Before the end of the year, Ponce de León had established a small settlement near this port on a hill he called Caparra.

Ponce de León returned to Hispaniola sometime in early 1507 to check on his plantation and resume his governorship of Higüey. He remained there for about a year before again asking for permission to return to Puerto Rico. Both Governor Ovando and King Ferdinand were pleased with the gold he had brought back from the island. So they readily consented, authorizing him to conquer and settle the island for Spain.

By the time this map was made some seventy-eight years after Ponce de León's death, Puerto Rico was a thriving colony.

Puerto Rico—Island of Riches

Ponce de León's rich island saw some of its best days as a Spanish colony under his leadership. Later Spanish rulers lacked his abilities as an administrator and military leader and were ill prepared to meet the many challenges the island faced.

While the Arawak people were virtually exterminated by the mid-1500s, the Caribs, their warlike neighbors to the east, continued to raid homes and towns along the coast. Other European powers—the English, Dutch, and French—also attacked in several failed efforts to take over the Spanish possession. Hurricanes and epidemics added to the setbacks, killing many early settlers through the 1700s. Still, the island's Spanish population steadily grew. The sugar plantations, first started by Ponce de León, flourished, and coffee became a second major product starting in the 1700s.

Later, Puerto Ricans, people of Spanish descent born on the island, began to seek independence from Spain in the early 1800s. Several uprisings in the 1820s were put down, but the independence movement grew increasingly stronger by the 1850s. The Spanish government remained undecided on the issue until 1897, when it gave the Puerto Ricans a measure of control over their local government. One year later the Spanish-American War broke out, concluding with an American victory and an abrupt end to more than 350 years of Spanish rule. Today, Puerto Rico is a self-governing territory of the United States, known officially as a commonwealth.

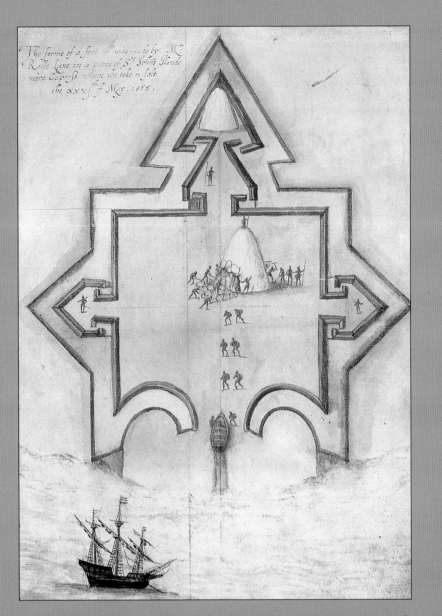

The forme of a fort th was made by Mr.
Ralfe Lane in a parte of St Johns Ilande
neere Cap̄ss where we toke in salt
the xxvij of May. 1585.

This illustration, made in the late 1500s, shows entrench-
ments, or a series of ditches, dug by Spanish settlers
around the walls of their coastal stronghold. Protection
was a necessity, as Spain's island holding was the target
of aggression from several fronts. Both the native residents of Puerto Rico and many of Spain's European rivals
launched attacks against the blossoming colony.

Ponce de León arrived back in Puerto Rico on August 12, 1508, with one ship and about fifty men. He built himself a permanent home for his family at Caparra with thick, whitewashed mud walls. As governor he put the Arawaks to work mining and farming. He even built a foundry to refine the gold they collected. Yet he realized that the long-term success of the island's economy rested on crops, not gold. He began cultivating sugarcane on his plantation, which remains the leading crop on Puerto Rico to this day.

But there was another man who longed to control Ponce de León's island. Christopher Columbus had died in Spain in 1506, a broken and disillusioned man. But Columbus's eldest son, Diego, was

Sugarcane proved a key product for the residents of Puerto Rico. By the time this landscape was painted in 1827, it had already become the island's most important crop.

determined to restore his father's name and make himself his rightful heir. He had wisely married into a powerful Spanish family and had great influence at court. Diego insisted that King Ferdinand make good on his promise to give control of the islands discovered by his father to the Columbus family. Unfortunately for Ponce de León, Hispaniola and Puerto Rico were two of those islands.

Diego Columbus arrived in Santo Domingo in July 1509 and took over the governorship of Hispaniola from Ovando. The king, however, had insisted Diego give Ponce de León a free hand in Puerto Rico. The conquistador, whose holdings in both San Juan and Hispaniola were making him rich and powerful, was resented by the son of the man he had once sailed with. In late October 1509, Columbus disregarded the king's orders and replaced Ponce de León as governor with his own man, Juan Cerón. Cerón was assisted by Miguel Díaz, who was named chief constable.

The king heard of Diego's actions and responded by sending a royal dispatch in which he insisted that Ponce de León be reinstated as governor, as well as named military captain and judge of the island. When the news reached the conquistador, he had Cerón, Díaz, and Díaz's deputy jailed and later sent back to Spain in chains. In retrospect, this might have been a rash move.

Governor once again, Ponce de León went to work to make Puerto Rico the showplace of the West Indies. A just governor, Ponce de León was well liked and respected by both Spaniards and Indians living on the island.

But his reign as royal governor was drawing to an unexpected end. Diego Columbus was furious with him for his treatment of his two lieutenants. This time King Ferdinand let Diego have his way. Diego confiscated Ponce de León's lands in Higüey and then sent Cerón and Díaz back to Puerto Rico to resume control of the government in 1511.

Diego Columbus
(1480–1526)

It is not easy to live in the shadow of a great father. Diego Columbus hoped to continue his father, Christopher's, legacy in the New World. For a while, he did. In 1511, after years of political infighting and maneuvering, Diego was granted his father's hereditary title of viceroy of the islands he had discovered. Diego, however, was no more of a capable administrator than his father. The Council of the Indies recalled him in 1523, and he was forced to defend himself from various charges of misgovernment. He died in obscurity in 1526 and was buried alongside his father in Valladolid, Spain. Diego's son Luis (c. 1521–1572) succeeded in gaining control of the island of Jamaica, another of his grandfather's discoveries. He also governed Hispaniola for eleven years but was banished to the North African city of Oran in 1565, where he died seven years later.

Christopher Columbus is pictured at home with his wife, dog, and his two sons, Diego and Luis.

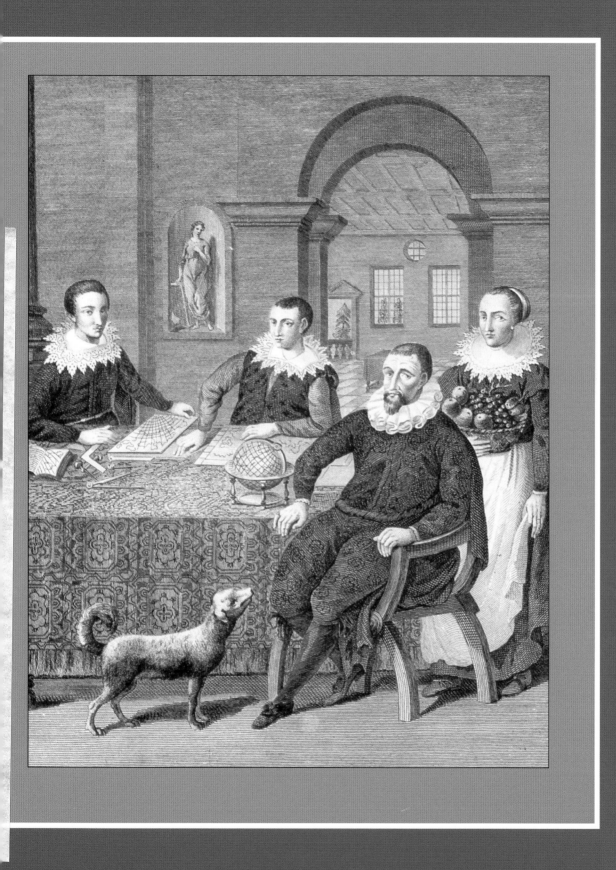

Ponce de León was forced to relinquish power once again. This time he watched helplessly as the inept Cerón and Díaz ruined much of what he had accomplished on Puerto Rico. While still the island's military captain, Ponce de León was not held in high regard by the new leaders and had little to do. Still in his thirties, he could not simply retire to his estate and lead the life of a gentleman of leisure. He craved adventure and new lands to explore. Again, his friends the Indians told him about a place more fabulous than Puerto Rico. It was the island of Bimini and it held, so they told him, the secret of eternal youth.

FIVE

The Fountain of Youth

At the beginning of the sixteenth century, the New World was still a largely uncharted region, believed to be full of unknown dangers and untold wonders. One of its most tantalizing lures was the island of Bimini. This huge, legendary land was said by the native peoples of the West Indies to be located north of the island of Cuba. It was not gold that made Bimini so attractive a destination but something even more precious—a fountain whose waters supposedly could restore "old men to youth."

The legend of the Fountain of Youth was one most Europeans were familiar with. It was a part of medieval folklore that had been passed on for hundreds of years. During biblical times, it was believed to exist in the Far East. But since many Europeans in the sixteenth century still thought that the New World *was* part of Asia, the fountain's supposed location in Bimini gained popular support.

Anxious to leave Puerto Rico, where he had been drained of his power and authority, Ponce de León wrote to King Ferdinand for permission to lead an expedition in search of Bimini. Did the explorer actually expect to find the Fountain of Bimini, as it was often called? Probably not.

Ponce de León was a clear-headed, practical soldier and administrator. He may have had a slight interest in the legend, but it was unlikely he

MAGICAL WATERS

The idea of a fountain or spring whose waters restored youth is as old as civilization itself. One of the first persons to search for this fountain was Alexander the Great, who conquered parts of Asia in the fourth century B.C.E. Like other seekers, Alexander believed the fountain was located in Asia and was fed by the waters of the Bible's Garden of Eden. Later Europeans believed the fountain was found on the Canary Islands off the northwestern coast of Africa. Christopher Columbus believed it lay in the West Indies somewhere between the island of Trinidad and the northeastern coast of South America.

Although these early explorers' beliefs may seem foolish to us today, they lived in times when life for many was short. The thought of waters that could rejuvenate or prolong life was irresistible.

In this woodcut, Ponce de León's men appear to have found the fountain of Youth in florida. In truth, they may not have looked very hard for it in the first place.

was obsessed with it. Besides, he was still a vigorous man in his thirties, hardly in need yet of the restorative powers of the fabled fountain. The person who more likely wanted the fountain's magic was King Ferdinand himself. In 1512 Ferdinand was sixty years old and in failing health. His queen, Isabella, had died eight years earlier, and the year after her death he had married Germaine de Foix, niece of Louis XII of France, who was thirty-five years his junior.

Ferdinand might indeed have longed to regain his youth by seeking the Fountain of Bimini. But he had other motives as well for granting Ponce de León a commission. For one, the king felt he owed the conquistador for his years of service to the crown. He was fully aware of his difficult position on Puerto Rico and was anxious to help him discover new lands he could govern. The king also knew any newly discovered territory would not be subject to the rule of Diego Columbus, whose power in the New World he wanted to curb. Previously uncharted land also meant more riches and revenue for the king.

The explorer received his commission in February 1512 but did not leave Puerto Rico for almost another year. He spent that time putting his affairs in order and preparing his expedition, while Cerón and Díaz did their best to harass him. At his own expense, he stocked three ships with supplies. Of the approximately sixty-five people who accompanied Ponce de León on the voyage, about half were sailors and half soldiers. There were also some Indians, a few blacks, and Juana Ruíz, the first European woman known to arrive in the present-day United States. The pilot of the lead ship was Antón de Alaminos, who had sailed with Christopher Columbus on his fourth and last voyage.

His crew assembled, on March 3, 1513, Ponce de León set sail from Puerto Rico for a fabled island that didn't exist. Instead he found a new continent—North America.

SIX

An Island Called Florida

Ponce de León sailed northwest from Puerto Rico toward the Bahamas. He stopped briefly at four small islands between March 9 and March 27. One of them was San Salvador, where Columbus had first landed in 1492. He then proceeded north along the coast of present-day Florida and first landed about 175 miles (282 kilometers) south of present-day St. Augustine. Ponce de León and his men waded ashore on April 3, about a week after Easter. The exact spot where he landed is not known; regrettably no eyewitness account of the voyage has survived. It may have been near where Cape Canaveral lies today.

This newfound paradise with its lush vegetation was strangely empty. The Spaniards found no native peoples to greet them, nor any signs of gold or other natural riches. Nor did they find the Fountain of Bimini, although Ponce de León already had a good idea this new land, which he took to be a huge island, was not Bimini at all. Instead he named it *La Florida*, meaning "the flowered one."

He may have named it that for two reasons. Most likely, he was impressed by the many colorful flowers growing in the region. It was also the Easter season, known in Spain as the *Pasqua florida*, or the "feast of flowers." Wherever the name came from, Florida remains the oldest European place-name in the United States.

The Florida coast, with its lush vegetation, attracted many explorers after Ponce de León first encountered it.

COLUMBUS'S MISSED OPPORTUNITIES

It was fate that determined that Juan Ponce de León, and not Christopher Columbus, should discover Florida. On his first voyage in 1492, Columbus was headed for the Florida peninsula, although he didn't know it. Then on October 7 he changed course and turned his ships west-southwest. Instead of landing near present-day Fort Pierce on Florida's eastern coast, he landed on San Salvador instead.

The day he landed, October 12, Columbus wrote in his log: "Many of the men I have seen have scars on their bodies . . . they indicated that people from nearby islands come to San Salvador to capture them. . . . I believe that people from the mainland come here to take them as slaves." The invading people he was referring to were the Calusa, and their home was in southern Florida.

Two weeks later, Columbus discovered the island of Cuba to the southwest. When he sailed from Cuba he planned to travel west, but strong winds forced him to change his course again. So he sailed east and discovered Hispaniola instead. If the weather had been more favorable, Columbus would have continued west and almost certainly would have discovered Florida—two decades before Ponce de León did.

The three ships continued along the eastern coast of Florida, briefly heading north until a storm drove them south. Not far from their original landfall, they discovered an Indian village. The Indians greeted the new-comers and invited them to stay and eat with them. But they no sooner left to get food for the feast, when they attacked the Spaniards with their bows and arrows. The men escaped injury as they fled back to their ship, but it was a sobering discovery. The Indians of Florida would prove to be the most hostile and dangerous of any native peoples Ponce de León had yet encountered.

The expedition continued south along the coast, stopping at two inlets. Just before reaching the second, Lake Worth Inlet, the party made another unsettling discovery. Antonio de Herrera Tordesillas, who wrote one of the few contemporary accounts of Ponce de León's first voyage to Florida, described what the expedition encountered:

The native people that early explorers met in Florida were rarely as friendly as those shown in this 1563 engraving.

A River in the Ocean

Ponce de León's discovery of the Gulf Stream was just as important as his discovery of Florida. This major ocean current forms in the western Caribbean Sea and flows north through the Gulf of Mexico and the Strait of Florida, where Ponce de León first encountered it. It then moves up the coast to Nantucket Island where it flows east toward Europe. This "river in the ocean" moves as much as 4 billion tons (3.6 billion metric tons) of water per minute up to 5 miles (8 kilometers) per hour.

The discovery of the Gulf Stream changed the sea routes mariners followed to and from the New World. Antón de Alaminos, who first noted the current, advised Hernán Cortés, conqueror of Mexico, to send his gold shipments to Spain along the Gulf Stream in order to move them swiftly and outdistance the region's many pirate ships. The increased use of Gulf Stream trade routes established Havana, Cuba, as an important port and later helped the Spaniards to select St. Augustine, located near the Gulf Stream, as the site for their first settlement in mainland North America.

With the coming of steam power and steamships in the 1800s, the Gulf Stream played less of a critical role in North Atlantic travel. Ships using steam power could travel against the Gulf Stream, something the sailing ships of Ponce de León's day could not do.

This engraving from the late 1500s shows a village typical of Florida's native peopl[e]. Palisades, the often spiked poles that were lined up to form a wall, were a much-needed form of protection.

On the next day [April 21] they followed the coastline—all three ships—and they encountered a current that they were unable to sail against even though they had a strong wind. The two ships nearest to the shore anchored but the current was so strong that it made the cables [anchor chains] quiver.

What Tordesillas was describing was the ocean current known as the Gulf Stream. This powerful flow held the ships back, but as Ponce de León's pilot, Antón de Alaminos, who is credited with its discovery, recognized, the Gulf Stream could be used to advantage, especially by ships returning to Spain from the New World.

Ponce de León continued down the Florida coast, reaching Key Biscayne, one of the string of islands known as the Florida Keys, on May 12. Several days later he reached Key West, the island farthest from the mainland. He then set a course north up the west coast of Florida, arriving at present-day Charlotte Harbor near Sanibel Island on May 23. There

Ponce de León's Route, 1513

Atlantic

Ocean

FLORIDA

St. Augustine

Gulf of
Mexico

BAHAMAS

SAN SALVADOR

CUBA

DOMINICAN
REPUBLIC

HAITI

PUERTO RIC

JAMAICA

Caribbean Sea

THE CALUSA INDIANS—FIRST FLORIDIANS

The Calusa were fierce warriors who controlled south-western Florida at the time of Ponce de León's arrival. While warfare was a primary interest, there was a more productive and artistic side to these native people as well.

The Calusa were excellent fishermen who used both the land and the sea to their advantage. They raised turtles in stone pens and harvested oysters in lagoons that they had created themselves.

Their ability as wood carvers was not widely recognized until 1895, when their work was discovered in a swamp in Key Marco. Today these beautiful carvings are considered superior examples of Native American art.

The Calusa were ingenious builders, too. They constructed their capital, Calos, on a large mound of discarded seashells. Their island at Key Marco had terraced gardens, nine canals, and a small mound temple. From the relics and artifacts they left behind, it is clear that the Calusa were an accomplished and highly organized nation.

Florida's Calusa Indians were not only skilled at fishing but were also fine artisans and builders.

the party had its worst confrontation with the native Floridians. The Calusa Indians, a warlike people, attacked under the leadership of their *cacique*, or chief, Carlos. The fight lasted all day, ending with the Spaniards' retreat at nightfall.

Out of danger, the expedition headed southwest along the Gulf of Mexico. Ponce de León had learned much about Florida and was ready to return to Puerto Rico to make a full report to the king. On June 21, 1513, the expedition stopped at a small group of islands about 60 miles (97 kilometers) west of Key West. There they caught large turtles that would serve as food for the voyage home. Ponce de León called the islands the Tortugas, Spanish for "turtles." Today they are known as the Dry Tortugas.

Two of the ships, one carrying Ponce de León, arrived back in Puerto Rico on October 19, 1513. The third ship returned four months later, its crew claiming to have found the island of Bimini. (What they most likely found was Andros Island, the largest in the Bahamas.) It had a natural spring, according to ship's captain Juan Perez de Ortubia. But no matter how much water the crew drank from the spring, they did not grow one day younger. So much for the Fountain of Youth, but Ponce de León was not discouraged. The "island" of *La Florida* was a rich and fertile land that he was now anxious to settle.

S E V E N

The King's Favorite

Ponce de León returned to a Puerto Rico in a far worse state than when he had left it eight months earlier. The government, under Cerón and Díaz's poor leadership, was completely disorganized. Sensing weakness, the Carib Indians had attacked and looted homes along the shore in their huge war canoes, killing several colonists.

When Ponce de León informed the humbled and fearful Cerón that he was planning a trip to Spain to meet with the king, the governor begged him to ask the king for help. He wanted the king to send more soldiers to defend Puerto Rico from the Carib. The conquistador was willing to do so, but he was more intent on getting the king's approval of his further exploration and colonization of *La Florida*. Having lost his power in Puerto Rico, he didn't want some other ambitious explorer to stake a claim to the new land that he had discovered.

Quoniambet, leader of the Caribs, is pictured in this illustration from 1575. The Carib launched a desperate battle to retain control of their homelands, but to no avail. Spain proved too powerful an adversary.

Ponce de León stayed home with his family through the winter and then sailed for Spain in April 1514. Obtaining an audience with the king was not something that was easily accomplished. No other conquistador from the New World had ever met personally with his majesty. Ponce de León, however, had a powerful patron at court, his former master and good friend Pedro Núñez de Guzmán. Guzmán arranged the important meeting.

Ponce de León arrived at the Spanish port of Bayona at the end of April. He spent the summer traveling around his homeland and arrived in Seville in September to meet King Ferdinand at his court at Valladolid. He was probably shocked when he first saw the monarch. Once a strong and virile man, Ferdinand was now old and sick. He had less than two years to live.

Juan Ponce de León was the first conquistador to be knighted for his achievements in the New World. He was also given his own coat of arms by Spain's King Ferdinand.

Coat of Arms

The European tradition of the coat of arms can be traced back to early medieval times. This symbolic emblem was originally worn by a knight on his shield as a means of identifying him in battle. Later it came to represent the high social status of an entire family. Many coats of arms contained in their design an object or figure called a charge. It often was an animal or plant. A motto or brief text called the device was also often part of the design.

Ponce de León's coat of arms, bestowed on him by King Ferdinand, contained a shield divided in equal halves. The left half depicted three islands surrounded by waves set against a field of blue. The islands represented the lands Ponce de León had explored and governed—Puerto Rico, Florida, and the elusive Bimini. The right half of the shield pictured a red lion standing on its hind legs, symbolizing the family of León. Above the shield was a helmeted head, possibly representing Ponce de León's bravery in war.

Being granted a personal coat of arms was an honor that long outlived the conquistador. It became the symbol of his family and its status on the island of Puerto Rico for generations to come.

The skills of Amerigo Vespucci, seen here as a young man, were questionable. Many of his exploits in the New World were suspect and hard to verify. His talent for self-promotion, however, led to two continents—North and South America—being named in his honor.

The king was very pleased with Ponce de León and his discovery. He may have been disappointed that de León was unable to confirm the existence of the Fountain of Youth, but his descriptions of the lush paradise of *La Florida* more than made up for it. The king also wanted to reward the conquistador for his long and faithful service on Puerto Rico.

Ferdinand knighted his visitor, bestowing on him the title of don, or sir. He also gave Ponce de León his own coat of arms, an honor few Spaniards received. The king made his esteemed subject captain-general for life in Puerto Rico, a member of the city council, and a chief justice. Most important of all, de León was granted a new contract to conquer Florida and settle it. He would be *adelantado*, or governor, of Florida as well as the island of Bimini, which the king still hoped he might find.

But the monarch's generosity came with a condition. Before he could return to Florida, Ponce de León was charged with ridding Puerto Rico of the Carib. The king gave him an armada of three ships to help accomplish this, but it was up to Don Juan to carry out the task successfully. He was to carry the fight directly to the Carib-occupied islands to the east and north of Puerto Rico.

While in Seville, Ponce de León met several other explorers, including Sebastian Cabot, who had reached Hudson Bay in 1508 and sailed along the eastern coast of present-day Canada and the United States. He also talked with Juan Vespucci, whose late uncle Amerigo claimed to have explored the American mainland in 1497. Despite controversy about whether he actually made this voyage, Amerigo Vespucci was honored with having his name, not Columbus's, given to the new continent of America.

Between his meetings with fellow explorers and preparing his three ships for their mission, six months had passed before Ponce de León was ready to return to the New World. Finally on May 14, 1515, he set sail to undertake his most challenging assignment to date.

EIGHT

At War with the Carib

Ponce de León found himself at war with the Carib even before returning to Puerto Rico. On the way there, he stopped at the island of Guadeloupe. There are at least two versions of what happened next. According to one, the conquistador sent ashore a group of washer-women, who were escorted by a band of soldiers. No sooner had they arrived on the island than they were attacked by a Carib war party with poisoned arrows. The warriors killed the soldiers and took the women captive. Ponce de León panicked on seeing the attack from his ship and took to sea at once, leaving the women behind.

Another version of the Carib attack claims that no women were sent ashore and that though some men were wounded, all were rescued. Ponce de León's flight, according to this version, was strategically the only sensible course of action. The truth behind this incident may never be known, but it seems unlikely, given the conquistador's military record, that he would have abandoned anyone, especially unarmed women, and run from a fight.

Whichever story is true, the incident did not shake Ponce de León's resolve to rid his island of the dreaded Carib. He finally reached Puerto Rico on July 15, 1515. Some time after, he sent a fleet of ships commanded by Captain Iñigo de Zúñiga to the group of small islands to the south known as the Lesser Antilles. (Puerto Rico, Jamaica, Hispaniola, and Cuba made up the Greater Antilles.)

Ponce de León continued his campaign against the Carib for several years. Regrettably, like the remaining five years of the explorer's life,

The ability of the Carib Indians to resist the onslaught of Europeans in their traditional homelands was due, in large part, to their fierce, warlike nature.

this time is poorly documented. There are few details of the struggle. It must have been a frustrating experience for the veteran soldier, for the Carib lived across an area of more than 1,000 miles (1,609 kilometers) covering countless islands in the Lesser Antilles. Ponce de León may have given up on the goal of eradicating them and settled for simply defending Puerto Rico from their attacks.

He must have also been frustrated by political developments on Puerto Rico. A new governor, Sancho Velazquez, took power in November 1514 and served for five years. Although a more capable administrator than Cerón, Velazquez felt threatened by Ponce de León and remained unfriendly and uncooperative throughout his time there.

In 1516 news reached the New World that King Ferdinand had died. He was succeeded by his sixteen-year-old grandson Charles I. Ponce de León worried whether the new king would fulfill the promises made to the explorer by his grandfather concerning *La Florida*. So Ponce de León decided to return to Spain to restate his claims to the region. Although there is no record of it, it is believed that his wife, Leónor, died sometime before he left Puerto Rico.

Ponce de León arrived in Spain on November 16, 1516. Little is known about what happened during the eighteen months he remained there. His commission from Ferdinand regarding Florida seems to have been renewed, and he married a second time. His new wife was Juana de Pineda of Seville.

He arrived back in Puerto Rico with his new bride in May 1518. The island had undergone more changes in his absence. Governor Velazquez wanted to move the capital from the unhealthy swamp-infested Caparra to the nearby harbor, a better location for trade. Ponce de León opposed the move, but he was outvoted. The new town was soon called San Juan and the island of San Juan Bautista, for the first time, was officially known as Puerto Rico, the name

THE CANNIBAL CARIB—FACT OR FICTION?

The Carib were the most warlike of the three Indian groups that lived in the West Indies during the time of the conquistadors. (The other two native groups were the Arawak and the Ciboney.) They originally came from the northeastern coast of South America and the Amazon River valley. Around 1000 C.E. they migrated in long canoes across the Caribbean Sea, which was named for them, to the West Indies. There they went to war against the more peaceful Arawak and later the Spanish.

The Carib were reputed to be cannibals who ate the captive males of other tribes. It was said they believed by eating these warriors they would take on their courage and strength. Lurid, graphic stories spread about how the Carib bred female captives and fattened their male children in pens until they were ready to be eaten.

It is doubtful the Carib were as terrible as the Spaniards made them out to be. There is no evidence they were cannibals. The false belief that they were, though, helped the Spaniards to justify their extermination. Whatever the truth may be, the Indians' very name has been forever linked to this dreadful practice. When Christopher Columbus first encountered the Carib he mistakenly called them "Canibales." The old Spanish word *can*, means "dog." The Carib, many Spaniards believed, were more like dogs than humans, and so they continued to call them cannibals. Today only a few hundred Carib remain in the Caribbean and South America.

Carib Indians, shown here torturing and killing a Franciscan monk, were the subject of false impressions and wildly inaccurate portrayals. No evidence supports the claim they were cannibals.

As the years passed, Ponce de León found himself with little power
in Puerto Rico, the colony he was the first to govern.

Ponce de León himself had given to the harbor on first seeing it. Although he was largely responsible for the successful settlement of the island colony, the conquistador now felt less and less a part of it.

In the seven years that had passed since he had first explored *La Florida*, other Spaniards had ventured to its shores. Mapmakers had placed it on their maps, indicating it was not an island but a peninsula. But for Ponce de León it was still an island and would remain so in his mind until the day he died.

By 1520 the New World was buzzing with news of the ongoing conquest of Mexico and the Aztec Empire by conquistador Hernán Cortés. It made Ponce de León all the more eager to begin his own conquest of Florida. There was little left to keep him in Puerto Rico. His second wife had died, his son had moved to Hispaniola, and his daughter Isabel had married the new governor of Puerto Rico, Antonio de la Gama. He was ready to return to the still unknown land where he hoped to gain his greatest fame and glory.

N I N E

To Die in Florida

The preparations for Ponce de León's second voyage to Florida were much more trying than the first. This time he was not going simply to explore new land and to fight Indians but to establish a permanent settlement. This meant more supplies would have to be stowed to provide food for the some two hundred settlers who would be the first to live in the new colony. It would be a while before they could grow their own food. Seeds, essential to their survival, were packed aboard as was livestock and fifty horses to be used for labor and transportation. Craftsmen and other workers were recruited to build shelters and homes, while priests and missionaries were included in an attempt to convert the Indians to Christianity. Conversion was seen as an important part of the Spaniards' mission in the New World.

Shortly before sailing, Ponce de León wrote a letter to King Charles, who by then was called Charles V of the Holy Roman Empire. "I am returning to that Island [Florida], if it pleases the will of God, to settle [it]," he wrote, "being able to carry enough people to be able to do it, because there the name of Jesus Christ may be spoken, and Your Majesty may be served by the agricultural production of that land."

This letter is unfortunately one of the few surviving documents about Ponce de León's second voyage to Florida. Only two other letters, one of them written to a cardinal in Spain, refer to the voyage. Later chroniclers, such as Bartolome de Las Casas, barely mention the

Although his men carried their fallen leader to safety after an attack by Indians in Florida, Ponce de León would not recover from his wound and died shortly after in Cuba.

voyage, and their accounts are filled with inaccuracies. For example, Las Casas gives the year of the expedition as 1512, one year before Ponce de León's first voyage to Florida!

What we do know with some certainty is that Ponce de León sailed from Puerto Rico on February 20, 1521, with two ships and arrived on the west coast of Florida several weeks later.

He may have chosen the west coast as an ideal location to settle because it was closer to Cuba, another Spanish colony, and newly conquered Mexico. Exactly where he landed is not known, but it is believed to be in the vicinity of present-day Fort Myers, between Charlotte Harbor, where he had previously landed, and the Caloosahatchee River.

From the March landing through June, the Spaniards probably explored the area and may have begun to build their settlement. Their confrontations with the Calusa Indians were violent. There were probably skirmishes throughout this time. The fighting came to a head about July 1, 1521.

Where the final battle occurred is unknown. It may even have taken place at sea, since the Calusa, like the Carib, were excellent canoeists. Wherever it took place, the fighting was fierce. The Spaniards were overwhelmed by the Indians and their poisoned arrows. Many of them were killed. Ponce de León was struck in the thigh with an arrow. His nephew, Hernán Ponce de León, was also seriously wounded.

The wounded leader eventually gave the order to flee to Cuba in the ships. During the voyage, Hernán died and was buried at sea. His uncle survived the trip, but his untreated wound became seriously infected. Ponce de León lingered a few days after arriving in Havana and then died. He was forty-seven years old. One of his last commands was to sell all his goods on board and use the money to buy horses to be sold to the Spaniards in Mexico. The profits from the sale were to be sent to his family.

The governor of Cuba arranged an elaborate funeral for the honored conquistador, who was buried in Havana. Thirty-eight years later, his grandson, Juan Ponce de León II, had his remains brought to Puerto Rico and laid in a sepulcher in the church of San José in San Juan. The body was moved again in 1909 from the church to a marble tomb in San Juan Cathedral.

The epitaph on the tomb, written by historian Juan de Castellanos, reads:

"Here rest the bones of a Lion mightier in deeds than in name."

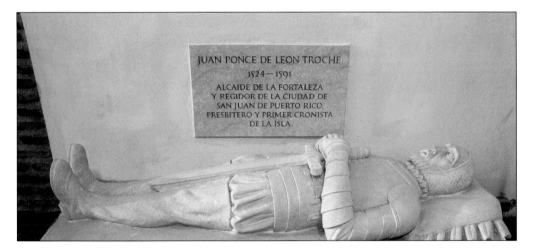

Ponce de León's left a long legacy in the New World. Many family members are buried in Puerto Rico, including this relative who was an alcaide, or military commander, in San Juan.

PONCE DE LEÓN'S "WHITE HOUSE"

Casa Blanca, or "white house," was begun by Ponce de León's son-in-law Juan García Troche in San Juan in 1521. It was to be a home for the conquistador, but he died before it was finished. The house was destroyed by a hurricane two years later and then rebuilt of sturdier stone and cement.

The descendants of Juan Ponce de León lived in *Casa Blanca* for more than 250 years. It is the oldest continuously occupied residence in the Western Hemisphere. In 1779 it was taken over by Spanish military leaders, and in 1898 it became a residence for American military commanders when the United States seized the island from Spain after the Spanish-American War.

Today the house is a national historic monument and a museum containing artifacts from the first 300 years of its long and colorful history.

Ponce de León did not live long enough to reside in Casa Blanca, the house built for him in San Juan, Puerto Rico. But generations of his descendants did. Today de León's "White House" is a museum.

Afterword

Juan Ponce de León is perhaps still "mightier in deeds than in name" to this day. He is the most misunderstood of the great Spanish conquistadors. He did not find, or perhaps even seek, a fountain of youth. He did not found St. Augustine, Florida, which many mistakenly associate with him. The sad truth is, he did not live long enough to establish any settlement in Florida.

Still, Ponce de León was the first European to discover and explore Florida and blazed the way for many of the explorers who followed him. Vázquez de Ayllón set up the first named European settlement north of Florida in what is now Georgia only five years after Ponce de León's death. This community lasted only two months, but two other settlements were established in Florida by the Spanish at Pensacola in 1559 and by the French at Fort Caroline in 1564. The following year the Spanish founded St. Augustine, the only one of these to succeed, and drove the French from Fort Caroline.

First Permanent Settlement in America

Spanish explorer Pedro Menéndez de Avilés founded St. Augustine in 1565. Avilés established the town on the northeastern coast of Florida at the site of an old Indian village. He named it for St. Augustine because he discovered it on the saint's feast day.

St. Augustine soon became Spain's military headquarters in North America. As such, it had a violent history. In 1586 English buccaneer Sir Francis Drake looted and burned the town. English colonists from South Carolina attacked St. Augustine in 1702, and settlers from Georgia did the same in 1740. Both times the Spaniards were able to repel the English.

Finally in 1763 Spain gave St. Augustine and the rest of Florida to England in exchange for Cuba, which the English had captured the previous year during the French and Indian War. Spain had been France's ally in that conflict. Spain regained control of Florida twenty years later and held it until 1821, when it was taken over by the United States. It became the twenty-seventh state in 1845.

While much of Florida has few traces of its Spanish past, St. Augustine's old town still has many historic buildings and homes that are charming reminders of more than 230 years of Spanish rule and culture. The popular tourtist attaction, the Fountain of Youth, however, was built in modern times and has, sad to say, no power to reverse the aging process.

Afterword

Although it was slow to be settled due to its aggressive native peoples and a lack of gold, Florida eventually fulfilled the promise envisioned by its discoverer back in 1513. Today it is one of the most populous states and a leader in agriculture and tourism.

But to find Ponce de León's greatest achievement one has to look to Puerto Rico. The fourth-largest island in the Caribbean, it was founded, conquered, and settled due largely to the efforts of this one man. His importance to the island's history is reflected in the many ways he is remembered there

This statue in San Juan is just one of the many memorials to Juan Ponce de León found on the island of Puerto Rico.

today. Of the 150 Spanish governors Puerto Rico had until its annexation by the United States in 1898, none is recalled with anything approaching the honor, respect, and even love shown to Juan Ponce de León. An impressive statue of him stands in San Juan in the plaza facing the church of San José where his body once lay. His tomb in the cathedral in San Juan is an island landmark. The Avenida (Avenue) Ponce de León is one of the main thoroughfares in San Juan. And the city of Ponce, the second largest in Puerto Rico, is also named in his honor.

Although known as a soldier fighting against the Moors in Spain and the Indians of the New World, Ponce de León was not the thoughtless slaughterer that Cortés, Pizarro, and other conquistadors were. It is true he exploited the Indians, growing rich on their labor, but he also tried to improve their lives and time and again sought to avoid unnecessary conflict with them.

More importantly, he was a conquistador who valued the fruit of the earth far greater than its mineral wealth. He had the foresight to see that long after the gold and silver of the Americas were exhausted, the land would continue to produce fruits, vegetables, and grains to feed the people not only of the New World but the Old World, too.

It is no wonder that King Ferdinand was more devoted to and supportive of Ponce de León than any of his other conquistadors. He must have seen greatness in him—a greatness that continues to be recognized today.

Juan Ponce de León and His Times

c. 1474   Ponce de León is born in San Tervas de Campos, Spain.

1492   He may have taken part in the Battle of Granada, driving the Moors out of Spain. Christopher Columbus makes his first voyage to the New World.

1493   Ponce de León most likely accompanies Columbus on his second voyage to the New World.

1502   He arrives on Hispaniola with new governor Nicolás de Ovando.

1504   He puts down the rebellion of the Arawak Indians in Higüey and is rewarded with the governorship of that province.

1506   He leads an expedition to Puerto Rico; Columbus dies in Spain.

1508   Ponce de León makes a second voyage to Puerto Rico and establishes a settlement.

1511   He is replaced as governor of Puerto Rico by Diego Columbus.

1513   He discovers Florida while searching for the island of Bimini.

1514   He returns to Spain where he is knighted by King Ferdinand and is given a commission to settle Florida.

1515   Ponce de León arrives back in Puerto Rico and launches a campaign against the fierce Carib Indians.

1516   King Ferdinand dies. Ponce de León returns to Spain to discuss his claim to Florida with Ferdinand's grandson King Charles I.

1518   He arrives back in Puerto Rico.

1521   He returns to Florida to establish a settlement and is seriously wounded in a battle with the Calusa Indians. He dies in Cuba a short time later.

1565   St. Augustine, Florida, is founded by Pedro Menéndez de Avilés.

1821   Florida becomes a territory of the United States.

Further Research

Books

Cardona, Rodolfo, and James Cockcroft. *Juan Ponce de León: Spanish Explorer*. Broomall, PA: Chelsea House, 1995.

Greenberger, Robert. *Juan Ponce de León: The Exploration of Florida and the Search for the Fountain of Youth*. New York: Rosen, 2003.

Harmon, Dan. *Juan Ponce de León and the Search for the Fountain of Youth* (Explorers of the New World series). New York: Chelsea House, 2000.

Heinrichs, Ann. *Ponce de León: Juan Ponce de León Searches for the Fountain of Youth* (Exploring the World series). Minneapolis, MN: Compass Point Books, 2002.

Manning, Ruth. *Juan Ponce de León* (Groundbreakers series). Chicago, IL: Heinemann Library, 2001.

Morley, Jacqueline. *Exploring North America*. Lincolnwood, IL: NTC Contemporary Publishing Company, 1996.

Sakurai, Gail. *Juan Ponce de León* (Watts Library of Exploration). New York: Franklin Watts, 2001.

Whiting, Jim. *Juan Ponce de León* (Latinos in American History series). Bear, DE: Mitchell Lane Publishers, 2002.

Videos

Ponce de León: The First Conquistador. A & E Home Video, VHS, 1995.

Further Research

Web Sites

Juan Ponce de León

http://www.newadvent.org/cathen/12228a.htm

http://www.fcps.edu/KingsParkES/technology/bios/deleón.htm

Other Conquistadors of Florida

http://www/floridahistory.org/floridians/conquis.htm#first

Puerto Rico

http://welcome.topuertorico.org/index.shtml

BIBLIOGRAPHY

Baker, Nina Brown. *Juan Ponce de León*. New York: Knopf, 1957.

Davis, T. Frederick. *History of Juan Ponce de León's Voyages to Florida*. Jacksonville, FL: T. Frederick Davis, 1935.

Fuson, Robert H. *Juan Ponce de León and the Spanish Discovery of Puerto Rico and Florida*. Blacksburg, VA: McDonald & Woodward Publishing Company, 2000.

Lawson, Edward W. *The Discovery of Florida and Its Discoverer Juan Ponce de León*. Nashville, TN: Cullum and Ghertner, 1946.

McKown, Robin. *The Image of Puerto Rico*. New York: McGraw-Hill, 1973.

Peck, Douglas T. *Ponce de León and the Discovery of Florida: The Man, The Myth, and the Truth*. St. Paul, MN: Pogo Press, 1993.

Source Notes

Chapter 4:

p. 25: "¡Que puerto tan rico!" Robin McKown, *The Image of Puerto Rico* (McGraw-Hill, 1973), p. 32.

Chapter 6:

p. 39: "Many of the men I have seen have scars . . ." Robert H. Fuson, *Juan Ponce de León and the Spanish Discovery of Puerto Rico and Florida* (McDonald & Woodward, 2000), p. 85.

p. 43: "On the next day they followed the coastline…" Fuson, p. 106.

Chapter 9:

p. 60: "…I am returning to that Island…" Fuson, pp.162-163.

p. 63: "*Here rest the bones…*" Ruth Manning, *Juan Ponce de León* (Heinemann, 2001), p. 38.

Index

Page numbers in **boldface** are illustrations.

75

Index